MW00682419

Preparing the Assembly to Celebrate

Kim Aldi - Wanner

NOVALIS
THE LITURGICAL PRESS

Design: Eye-to-Eye Design, Toronto

Layout: Suzanne Latourelle

Illustrations: Eugene Kral

Series Editor: Bernadette Gasslein

© 1997, Novalis, Saint Paul University, Ottawa, Ontario, Canada

Business Office: Novalis, 49 Front Street East, 2nd floor,
    Toronto, Ontario M5E 1B3

Published in the United States of America by The Liturgical
    Press, Box 7500, Collegeville, MN 56321-7500

Novalis: ISBN 2-89088-796-0

The Liturgical Press: ISBN 0-8146-2500-2
    A Liturgical Press Book
    Library of Congress data available on request.

Excerpts from the English translations of: *The Roman Missal* ©
    1973, International Committee on English in the Liturgy,
    Inc. Used by permission. All rights reserved.

Printed in Canada.

© 1997, Novalis. All rights reserved.

Canadian Cataloguing in Publication Data

Aldi-Wanner, Kim, 1949–

    Preparing the assembly to celebrate

(Preparing for liturgy)
    Includes bibliographical references.

ISBN 2-89088-796-0

    1. Religious gatherings — Catholic Church.
    2. Catholic Church — Liturgy.
    3. Public worship — Catholic Church. I. Title. II. Series

BX2230.2.A42 1997   264'.03   C97-900705-4

Contents

Introduction

If, on a typical Sunday morning, you were asked to turn to the people next to you in the pew and ask them why they came to mass, what response do you think you would receive? Many people would say they have come because coming to church on Sunday means something to them: a sense of belonging, a sense of community, a sense of God's presence. Others might like the music or the homily. Some people will say they have come out of a sense of obligation—because the church says that we have to go to church on Sunday. If you were to talk to some of the younger members of the assembly, they might tell you that they are in church because their parents made them come.

How many would respond that they are present because God has called them to come and celebrate with this community? We respond to God's call with praise and thanksgiving. Our ability to give praise and thanks to God always originates with God. This is echoed in the words of Eucharistic Prayer III: "from age to age you have gathered a people to yourself." It is our saying "yes" to God's call that makes us put the Sunday paper down, turn off the early morning sports, or decide that the lawn can be mowed or the snow shoveled at another time, in order that we may join with our brothers and sisters to offer praise and thanksgiving to the God who has called us. This is why the Second Vatican Council calls the liturgy the "source" and the "summit" of our lives as Christians *(Constitution on the Sacred Liturgy [CSL], 10)*.

The pattern of God's call and our response, the foundation of how we live out our daily lives as Christians, is most fully expressed when we gather for worship. The assembly that gathers together on Sunday or during the week to celebrate eucharist, the sacraments, or the prayer of the church becomes a visible sign to the world of God's loving presence, not only in the lives of this community, but for all people. The gathered assembly makes visible the body of Christ, the church. In spite of our sinfulness, the times when we have failed to be a visible presence of God in the world, we are still a people called by

God, through Christ, in the Spirit, to carry out God's mission in the world. We are called to make God present in a world where God often remains invisible, and where God's offer of grace is frequently rejected or ignored. Participation in the liturgy of the church helps to strengthen those who gather to bring the healing and compassionate presence of Christ into our world.

CHAPTER 1

The Assembly, a Community of Faith

If we are to be transformed by God's love, we need to continually strive to deepen our relationship with God. Some periods in history have been marked by a strong separation between the sacred and the secular, between the world that we live in, and the prayer and worship of the church. We have not yet completely overcome this division. For many of us, the time that we take to come to mass or celebrate the sacraments is "time out" from our ordinary lives. We come to church for mass on Sunday and then we return to living our lives. We do not always understand that God is experienced in the whole of our lives: in our work, in our families, in our community, in the whole of the creation that surrounds us. God is present to sustain us in our times of deep pain and sorrow, and is there to celebrate with us in our times of joy and happiness. God is with us in the ordinary events of our everyday lives. In the confusion of our fast-paced lives and the many distractions around us, God's constant and loving presence often goes unnoticed.

We do not live our daily life in isolation. We are born into a society, a culture, a family. We are social beings. Within this community we experience decisive moments of our life such as birth, marriage, illness and death. The community that we live in helps interpret these experiences for us. This interpretation helps us to accept or come to terms with these situations and to respond in a way that gives the experience some form or direction.

As human persons we are born into a family and a community. As Christians, we are baptized and born into a community of faith. We gather together because of our shared faith in the risen Christ. The conciliar documents emphasize that the sacraments are acts of faith (*CSL*, 59). They both require and presuppose faith. We experience God's loving presence through the persons and events of our lives. The sacraments then provide the medium to ritualize this experience of God in both the communal life of the church and in its individual members at particular moments such as baptism, marriage and reconciliation. Our experience of God's love and forgiveness surrounds us from birth and continues to sustain us long after the celebration of the particular sacraments. Active participation in the ritual action of the faith community provides us with a medium through which we may encounter and celebrate this presence and action of Christ in our daily lives. Sacraments, therefore, are not isolated moments in the life of the Christian, but are part of a larger process.

Faith

What is this faith that we as Christians celebrate in the sacraments and endeavour to live out in our everyday lives? Faith is something that all human beings share; everyone lives by some form of faith. In trying to make sense of their life experience, human beings must believe that their way of life is best for them. For Christians this "basic human faith" must give way to the faith of the church, faith in Jesus Christ. This faith must be more than a lesson that has been learned from someone or from the catechism. It must be a living and dynamic faith that has its foundation in our life experience. For example, those brought up in the pre-Vatican II church can remember "learning" the faith by memorizing the catechism. Converts during this period also received "instruction" in the faith, usually on an individual basis from the parish priest. However, this is not enough, for faith moves us beyond this form of religious practice. Conversion, a commitment to living gospel values, becomes a life-long journey.

Christians, called to conversion at every stage of life, are a people who answer "yes" to God's call. Their lives are shaped by the example of Christ, who entrusted the totality of his life to the Father, even to dying on the cross and being raised from the dead. Therefore, for the sacraments to be truly life-giving, this faith needs to develop and grow. Through the action of faith, we allow our lives to be taken up in the process of God's self-communication, and be transformed. Within the community of the church, the people of God, the body of Christ, we publicly celebrate, in faith, God's action in our lives. We celebrate this presence in many ways: reconciliation, laying on of hands, water bath, bread and wine. Sacraments make visible for us what we celebrate—the presence of Jesus, reaching out and touching others. This means that when the community comes together to give thanks and praise to God, it should experience God's presence.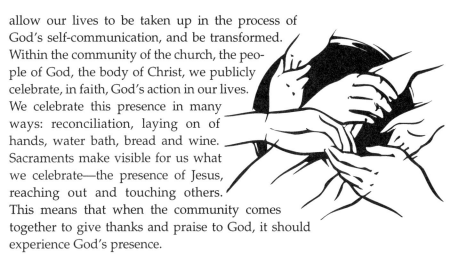

Experiencing God in Communal Worship

We believe that Christ is present and active in the liturgy in diverse ways: in the gathered assembly, in the word proclaimed, in the presiding minister, in the eucharistic species (*CSL,* 7). Christ, as high priest, is the source of communication that takes place in the liturgy as the mediator from God to the community of faith, and from the community of faith to God. Christ is the principal speaker and actor of the church's action (*Constitution on the Church* [*LG*], 21). Through Christ in the power of the Spirit, we carry out our ministry in the assembly. Active participation in sacramental action enables us to become more Christ-like, more human. At the same time it is operative in making the church a visible sign or sacrament of Christ's dynamic presence in the world.

Through the structure of call and response in the liturgical celebration, the community expresses its faith in the Triune God and gives thanks and praise for God's action in the life of the church and the world. The members of the assembly are called to incarnate in their lives what they promise in the liturgy. Through participation in the death and resurrection of Christ, they are impelled to reach out to family and community as an effective sign of God's saving love in the world. The community of faith is called to respond to God's call, to live as the people of God, the body of Christ.

Connecting with Believers over the Ages

The liturgy we celebrate today contains both a future and a past dimension. Every time we pray the "Our Father" we pray for the coming of God's kingdom. The reign of God that Jesus preached is present in our midst, but has not yet come to fulfillment. As Christians we continue to wait in joyful expectation until Christ comes again in glory.

The liturgy connects us with the assembly of believers from ages past. We pray: "From age to age you gather a people to yourself so that from east to west a perfect offering may be made to the glory of your name" (Eucharistic Prayer III). In telling the story of our history as God's people, we see how we have been shaped and transformed throughout the centuries by the saving power of God. Just as every age and culture hands on a heritage of prayer, music, ritual and symbol, so we too will pass on a legacy of prayer and worship for those who follow. This means that liturgical celebrations are not private acts belonging to individual Christian communities. They are "celebrations belonging to the whole Church, which is the 'sacrament of unity,' namely, the holy people united and ordered under their bishops" (*CSL*, 26).

At the same time the liturgy must speak to diverse Christian communities, draw people into the mystery of Christ and help them experience the saving power of God in their lives. We must know and understand our past in order to enrich our symbols and renew our rituals in ways that will enable our assemblies to enter into God's reign in the present. Then, with faith and hope, we will participate in the transformation of our world while awaiting that new creation where the fullness of God's "peace will be revealed" and God will "gather people of every race, language, and way of life to share in the one eternal banquet with Jesus Christ the Lord" (Eucharistic Prayer for Masses of Reconciliation II).

In Summary

1. Christian liturgy draws upon the experience of God in the daily lives of the baptized who come to celebrate in praise and thanksgiving the action of God in their lives.

2. Through our active participation as members of the assembly in the prayers and rituals of the church's worship our faith is deepened and the relationship between the members of this faith community and the faith community with God are renewed and strengthened.

3. At the end of our Sunday celebration we are told: "Go in peace to love and serve the Lord." As members of the Christian assembly we continue to give thanks and praise for God's saving action in our lives by living out in our daily life what we have just promised in the liturgy.

4. Our mission is to bring the Good News of salvation to our families, workplaces, political structures, local and parish communities. We are called to transform the world we live in through our Christian vocation "because the world itself is destined to glorify God the Father in Christ" (John Paul II, *Christifideles laici*, 15).

Discussion Questions

1. Does the liturgy that we celebrate in our parishes reflect the faith and life experience of the people who gather?

2. Does the manner in which we pray help the community to experience the presence of God and the sacredness of their everyday life?

3. When planning our liturgical celebrations, how do we balance the riches of our traditions while allowing our symbols and rituals to speak to various peoples in a diversity of cultures?

4. If we add symbols and rituals to our celebration, are they always "in keeping with the true and authentic spirit of the liturgy" (*CSL*, 37)? Can they bear the weight of the mystery that we celebrate?

CHAPTER 2

The History and Ministry of the Assembly in Scripture

Blow the trumpet in Zion; sanctify a fast; call a solemn assembly; gather the people (Joel 2:15).

Who is this people that God has called? The scriptures tell the story of how God has acted in their lives. We call this the history of our salvation. From the very beginning God had a plan for the whole of creation. We take an active role in salvation history by the way we respond to God's call. Our understanding today of the church as the people of God has its roots in the Old Testament.

Assembly in the Old Testament

The word used for assembly in the Old Testament is *qahal*, which means a gathering or a community that has been called together (Deuteronomy 5:22; Exodus 12:16; Numbers 20:4; Psalm 149:1). The term *qahal YHWH* means the assembled people of God. God and the Jewish people are united in a covenant relationship. The people belong to God, their creator and provider (Hosea 2:21-23). God demands that the Jewish people worship one God, observe certain standards set by their system of religious worship and keep the ten commandments. In return the Lord God will be their God, assisting and delivering them from all their enemies. Israel's great day of assembly occurred on Mount Sinai when they entered into a covenant with their God. Whenever the people accepted what God asked of them, they renewed this covenant.

The word of God was effective and carried power (Isaiah 55:8-11). The prophets conveyed God's word through the law, which provided God's people with direction on how to live out the covenant. The gathered assembly not only looked at the past and the present, but also at the future when God's plan for salvation would be fulfilled, and God would gather to God's self all the nations of the earth (Psalm 98:4-9; Isaiah 44:22; 53:10).

The temple in Jerusalem eventually became the centre of the Jewish religion with the assembly as its focal point. However, by the time of Jesus, the original sense of the universality and equality of the assembly was often lost. The assembly had become restricted by exaggerated rules and laws which governed what was pure and impure (Leviticus 4:13-21; 16:4; 21:18; Numbers 19:19-22). In the New Testament we find Jesus reacting to the restrictions which separated the people from their loving God (Matthew 23:1-36).

Assembly in the New Testament

The Old Testament between God and the Israelites is fulfilled in the New Testament. Through his life, death and resurrection, Jesus becomes God's revelation to the Christian community (John 14:9; Matthew 11:27). The God of the Old Testament is revealed in the historical person of Jesus Christ. The Word of God is Jesus (John 1:14). Everything that was true of the word in the Old Testament is true of Jesus. Jesus is effective, living, and dynamic—the creating Word of God. Through Jesus Christ God will gather all the nations to himself. This universal gathering will welcome the blind, the lame, women, children, sinners and tax collectors. No political, economic, or social barriers will divide God's people: neither Gentile or Jew, servant or free, woman or man (Galatians 3:28).

In the New Testament the centre of the assembly shifts from the temple to the person of Christ and his truth (John 2:18-22; 4:23-26). In the New Testament the blood of Christ establishes the covenant for all people and for all times (1 Corinthians 11:25-26).

The New Testament identifies the people of God as the church. The Hebrew *qahal YHWH* is translated by the Greek word *ekklesia* which means to "call forth." *Ekklesia* distinguishes the new people of God (1 Peter 2:10), the community of believers who gathered together in the name of Christ. The church of the New Testament was also described as the body of Christ (1 Corinthians 12:12-31). People entered the church through baptism, and were drawn into the mission of the church—to carry out Jesus' ministry in the world.

The Ministry of Jesus and the Ministry of the Assembly

Every baptized Christian has a ministry to carry out in the church. St. Paul in his letter to the Corinthians tells us that "there are varieties of gifts, but the same Spirit; and there are varieties of services, but the same Lord; and there are varieties of activities, but it is the same God ... Now you are the body of Christ and individually members of it" (1 Corinthians 12). This means that ministry is a part of our whole Christian experience, in our worship as well as in our daily lives. Our ministry at church on Sunday should reflect how we carry on Jesus' ministry in the world around us.

As Christians we are not part of the church to look out for our own needs, but to be a part of the community that carries on the work of the risen Lord in the world. Any truly authentic Christian ministry must continue what Jesus did in his public ministry here on earth.

What was Jesus' ministry? It consisted primarily in teaching and healing. Jesus always acted for God; he always followed the will of the Father. Jesus' service to the people whom he encountered was a sacrament of God's own service to these people. He always acted for God in meeting the needs of those around him. He was truly interested in the people who came to him and showed concern for their needs. There was so much suffering, pain and brokenness in the lives of people that Jesus' ministry was one of deep compassion: he truly suffered with his brothers and sisters. He tried to fight against the evils and oppression that enslave us as human beings: physical disability, poverty, hunger, political and social oppression, physical, and psychological disorders (Luke 6:20-37). He spent his life healing people. Jesus also taught about the kingdom of God and how we can enter into God's reign. He challenged everyone to conversion and repentance (Luke 7:36-50; 19:1-10). By eating with tax collectors and sinners, Jesus destroyed the barricades that block the relationship that exists between God and humanity (Mark 2:15-17; Luke 15:1-32).

The summit of Jesus' ministry was his death and resurrection through which he revealed the depth of the Father's love for the world. Jesus freely chose to experience suffering and death out of love for us. He readily absorbed the evil and hostility that were directed against him and, therefore, overcame the power of evil in the world (John 13:1). Jesus, as the sacrament of divine love, modeled for us how we can overcome the power of sin and evil in our own lives and in the whole of creation. How is this ministry reflected in our liturgical celebrations?

Ministry for the Sake of God's Reign

All ministry in the church exists for the sake of the reign of God. The church's mission is to carry on the proclamation of the kingdom through word, worship, witness and service. All members of the church, by reason of baptism and confirmation, are obliged to carry out this mission in their own lives. The community itself, not just individuals, needs to be forgiving, compassionate and reconciling. Just as Jesus in his humanity is the sacrament of God in the world, so too the church, as the Body of Christ, becomes the sacrament of Christ in the world. God's presence is the most visible when this community of God's people gathers together to celebrate the sacraments, especially the eucharist. Called by God's Spirit, the community gathers to give thanks and praise to the Father through the mediation of Jesus. God always hears our prayer because our prayer is made through Christ, in the Spirit. We always worship through Christ, with Christ, and in Christ. God is the primary focus of our worship—not us. Worship must always lead us to God.

There is something askew when the focus is on us as individuals, on how we feel, or what we like. Jesus did not say we had to love our neighbour only when it felt good. It was part of the law: love your Lord and your God, and love your neighbour as yourself (Matthew 19:16-19). The call to worship stems from our baptismal commitment: "it is our duty and our salvation, always and everywhere," to give God thanks and praise (Preface, Eucharistic Prayer II).

In Summary

1. From the beginning of time God had a plan for the whole of creation. The story of how we as God's people have a role in this plan is the history of our salvation.

2. We learn from the stories of the Old Testament how God fashioned a people and entered into a covenant relationship with them. This covenant relationship forms the basis of our Christian assembly today.

3. The covenant between God and God's people was fulfilled in Christ. The ministry and mission of the church today is to continue the ministry of Christ.

4. Baptism, our entering into the death and resurrection of Christ, is the foundation for all ministry in the church. Through baptism, we share in the priesthood of Christ.

5. We have the responsibility to participate fully in the life and worship of the church and to carry out the ministry of Christ in the world.

Discussion Questions

1. In your parish, does your ministry of assembly at church on Sunday reflect how you carry out Jesus' ministry in the world around you?

2. In your parish, does your community's ministry of assembly reflect Jesus' ministry in the world?

3. What must you do to improve the ministry of your assembly?

4. What must your community do?

CHAPTER 3

The Assembly in the Church's Worship

The Greek word for people, *laos*, becomes "laity" when translated into English. Until about the fourth century the only distinction that *laos* implied was that between the elect, who were God's people, and those who were not. Laity, therefore, was not used hierarchically to define those who were not ordained as opposed to those who were. The whole community played an active role in both church administration and ministry, along with a great diversity of ministries, both lay and ordained: bishops, elders, presbyters, deacons, readers, caretakers, singers, assisting ministers, widows. This changed between 250 and 400 A.D. when the role of laity in worship began to diminish. By the end of the middle ages, church ministry was reduced to the ordained clergy and their assistants. The people of God were divided into two classes: the laity, who held secondary status, and the clergy, who held the positions of leadership. This continued until the renewal brought about by the Second Vatican Council.

How did we move from the New Testament vision of church, in which the whole community shared in the mission and ministry of Jesus, to a community marked by divisions between the sacred and the secular, ordained and lay, from one in which the laity actively participated in the life of the church to one in which they were, mostly, passive spectators? In every age, the church exists and interacts with the political, social and economic forces that surround it. The structure, theology, ministry and worship of the Christian church has been changed both positively and negatively by the different ages. Therefore, the role of the "laity" in the structure and worship of the church can be traced through the impact of the different cultural and political shifts that have occurred during the various periods of the church's history.

Early Church

The roots of the eventual distinction between ordained and lay are found in the Constantinian church. The early church was a persecuted church; those members who sought baptism were motivated by deep faith and a strong sense of commitment. Through Constantine's Edict of Toleration in 313 A.D., and Theodosius' edict of Thessalonica in 380 A.D., Christianity became the official religion of the Roman Empire. The emperor took on the role of patron and protector of the Christian faith, closely connecting church and state. The church began to take on the trappings and structure of the Roman Empire. This led to the eventual distinction between ordained and lay in the worship of the church.

There was a shift from a variety of ministries, both ordained and charismatic, to the hierarchical organization of ministries based on the political structures of the Roman Empire. Many pagans converted, not out of a sense of faith or commitment, but because it was politically and economically astute to be a Christian. Even though Christianity was the official religion of the people, many kept their pagan superstitions. This also impacted on the worship of the church.

The barbarian invasions of the fifth century signaled the end of a united Roman Empire and the West was separated into various barbarian kingdoms. The church was left as the only institution that could safeguard both Roman civilization and Christian faith. There was little stability during this period. Wars, violence, poverty, famine, plagues, and the shifting balance of power affected church structures and influenced the repositioning of the laity to a secondary role.

Middle Ages

Monasticism eventually became the most stable element throughout the middle ages by providing a place for the preservation and development of both intellectual and spiritual thought. The monasteries also provided the framework that enabled the development of liturgy in such areas as the format for the daily office, liturgical chant, and architectural design to continue. Consequently, one of the most fundamental divisions of medieval life became the division that existed between the clergy and the laity. The laity, the majority of whom were illiterate, interpreted this to mean that salvation was only guaranteed to those who lived a religious life.

An even sharper distinction between the lay and religious life arose from the belief that, since the laity lived in the world and were involved in war, violence and sexual relationships, they would always be sinners. The state of holiness became associated with religious life and a wider gap developed between the world of the sacred and the world of the secular.

Worship Mirrors Social Structures

This development was reflected in the worship of the church. The domain of the sacred fell under the ordained ministry while the temporal belonged to the lay people. The clergy took over ministries that originally belonged to the laity. The worship of the church was conducted in Latin, a language that was understood by only some of the clergy. The priest turned his back to the people who then became mere spectators. During this period the priest began to pray the mass parts silently; by the end of the ninth century the eucharistic prayer was said in complete silence. The presider also took over all ministries including the readings and the chants that were normally sung by the choir.

Eventually, the power of the church became centralized in Rome. Gregory VII took a strong stand on the division between the authority of laity and clergy. Temporal matters belonged to the domain of the laity; only the clergy had authority in the realm of spiritual affairs. The laity, uneducated and distanced from the official prayer and worship of the church, developed their own religious piety. The continued use of Latin, now a foreign language, and their own sense of sinfulness and unworthiness even further removed them from participating in the eucharistic action. Their physical distance from the altar, architectural barriers, and the placement of clerical ministries in front of the assembly accentuated this. People now watched, rather than participated in, the liturgy.

The eleventh and twelfth centuries saw the rise of the universities as centres of learning. It was a period of theological development, when faith searched for another way of understanding and explaining the sacramental life of the church. The focus changed from a pastoral nature to one that was more concerned with formulating a precise definition of how sacraments functioned and what constituted their validity. By the thirteenth century, scholastic theologians had formulated a fairly precise definition of sacraments. Sacraments were codified into precise words and actions and centred more on the correct performance of the rite itself, than on the relationship between the individual, the community and God. For the average lay Christian the result of scholastic theology was the reduction of sacramental celebration to the bare essentials.

Consequently, instead of recognizing that God takes the initiative, people saw sacraments as means by which individuals earned salvation. If all the correct words were said and the accompanying actions performed at the proper time, then a person could "earn" the grace needed to get to heaven. There was a loss of the sense that sacraments were signs or symbols of the mystery of God, a mystery that can never be fully understood or explained.

The Reformation

Corruption within the church, lack of insight into the spiritual needs of the Christian people, the magic and superstition surrounding sacraments, and simony, the sale of indulgences, led to the Reformation. The Protestant Reformation also attacked abuses in the papacy and hierarchy of the Roman church, and, in doing so, emphasized the individual and the individual's relationship with God. In reaction to these attacks, the Roman church focused on the church as an institution, a perfect society. The resulting hierarchical model divided the church into two groups: the ordained or clerical office and the laity. Consequently, in sacramental practice the role of the ordained ministers gained significance as "dispensers of grace." Concurrently, the importance of the community was diminished and the role of the assembly was reduced even further. Catholics, during this period, became more concerned with obeying the law of the church than entering into a relationship with God through the communal prayer and worship of the church. This vision of church lasted until Vatican II.

Vatican II

The Second Vatican Council, the twenty-first ecumenical council of the Catholic Church, was called by Pope John XXIII. It began on October 9, 1962 and ended on December 8, 1965. Pope John realized that the developments of the modern world had changed our awareness of the relationship between the church and the world. He urged the Council to take on a pastoral direction; to make the church more timely and effective in the modern world. The church as a living body must continue to be relevant to people living in every age.

The Council's reflection began with the *Constitution on the Sacred Liturgy*. This document describes the liturgy as an indispensable medium by which "the faithful may express in their lives and manifest to others the mystery of Christ and the real nature of the true church" (*CSL*, 2). The liturgy is further represented as "the summit toward which the activity of the church is directed; at the same time it is the fount from which all the church's power flows" (*CSL*, 10). The Council also called for a renewal of all the sacramental rites.

The Council formulated some basic principles in the area of liturgical renewal: the importance of scripture in liturgical celebrations (*CSL*, 24); the use of the vernacular (*CSL*, 36); the role of music in liturgical celebrations (*CSL*, 112); the catechetical nature of the rites (*CSL*, 35); the communal dimension of liturgical celebrations with emphasis on the active participation of those present (*CSL* 21, 26, 27); and the restoration of the classical shape of the Roman liturgy, with its characteristic simplicity.

With this renewed theology of worship that comes to us from the Second Vatican Council, we understand liturgical celebrations as communal, public, and personal prayer, in which the church celebrates the paschal mystery: the life, death, resurrection and coming in glory of Jesus Christ. We gather together, and, through sign, symbol, word and sacrament, respond to God. Through the rites of the church, we give thanks for God's action in our lives, deepen our baptismal share in the dying and rising of Jesus Christ, and go forth to communicate the good news to others.

For the sacraments to authentically communicate the gospel message, these revised rites must both strengthen the faith of the church, and personally engage those whom God calls. When we attempt to apply these principles of liturgical renewal to our parish celebrations, we often fall short of the Council's vision. One of the reasons for this is that so called "traditional" and cultural aspects, which are unrelated to the faith and worship of the church, creep into our liturgies and take over. When this happens, the prayer and worship of the church as the action of the gathered community is weakened, and the community is in danger of losing sight of the presence of God as revealed through word and sacrament. To adapt the rites meaningfully for the present and for the future, we must understand the rite, the faith of the church, the role of the assembly, and be pastorally selective in adding traditional and cultural elements in our liturgy.

The Assembly: Primary Symbol

Since the close of the Council we have seen many external changes in the way the church prays and worships: the communion rail has been removed; the ritual books have been revised; lay people move back and forth from the sanctuary; and we pray in our own language and within our own culture. At the heart of the liturgical renewal was the recovery of the assembly as a primary symbol, and the phrase "full, conscious, and active participation" is the principle that rings out every time we gather to prepare or evaluate liturgy in our parishes.

Still, something appears to be missing. People speak of a loss of the sense of mystery, of the sacred. Some liturgy committees and planning groups search for "creative" ways to make the liturgy, as one group put it, "more user-friendly." We might ask the question: do we plan and prepare our liturgies for convenience or for how they make us feel? If we leave the liturgy feeling challenged and perhaps a bit uncomfortable, does that mean that it was not good worship? There are two sides to this question. Participation in the celebration should affirm us in our gratitude for all the blessings that God has given us. On the other hand, since we have not yet reached a state of perfection, we must be open to God's word confronting us with our need for repentance, challenging us to enter more deeply into the paschal mystery—the life, death, resurrection and coming again of Jesus Christ. We are transformed not only as individuals but as part of the assembly of people who share a common faith in Jesus Christ. In the waters of baptism, in the telling of the story of our salvation, in the breaking of bread, the laying on of hands, the anointing with oil, we come to experience in a concrete and tangible way that we are members of the living body of Christ. This assembly, who gathers Sunday after Sunday, becomes the primary symbol of our Christian liturgy, the icon of God's relationship with humanity and with the world.

Full, conscious, active participation

In most parishes on a given Sunday you will find people participating in the liturgy through song and the spoken prayers and petitions of the celebration. But "full, conscious, and active participation" is more than an external response; it means entering into the celebration with our "whole mind, body and soul." Liturgy does not just tell us about our covenant relationship as the people of God. It allows us to experience and deepen our relationship with God and God's creation, through Christ in the power of the Spirit, ever transforming us into the image and likeness of Christ. This continues to be our challenge today.

To encourage and enable the assembly to carry out an active ministry within the celebration, we have revised our ritual books, remodeled our churches, moved musicians out of choir lofts, and placed hospitality ministers at the door. These exterior changes are just the first step. Our interior attitude and understanding must also change. Although we speak of the importance of the assembly, the focus often remains the role and activity of the ordained and the official lay liturgical ministries in the liturgy. For example, every year parishes hold workshops and training sessions for ministries such as lectors, cantors, musicians, eucharistic ministers, and hospitality ministers. Do we hold workshops or training sessions for the ministry of the assembly? If we introduce the presider, lectors, eucharistic ministers, hospitality ministers, and musicians by name, what does this say about the importance of the rest of the assembly?

We often lose sight of the fact that the whole assembly celebrates. In the activity of the whole community we experience God in our celebrations. For "in the liturgy God is speaking to his people and Christ is still proclaiming his gospel ... And the people are responding to God by both song and prayer" (*CSL*, 33). We have truly participated in our eucharistic celebration when, open to the Spirit of God working within us, we carry our "Amen" to the world we live in. Sunday is not an isolated moment in the week. We are sent forth to rebuild relationships within our families and communities, to reach out to the poor and the oppressed, to be conscious of the needs of the people and the world that we live in, and to proclaim the Good News of salvation day after day, month after month, year after year.

We Are God's Instruments

Good liturgy is not magic. Good liturgy does not just happen. You can sing with a badly tuned piano but how much better the sound and the participation when the instrument is finely tuned. We are God's instruments. God's grace will still continue to work even if the liturgy is poorly enacted and ministers are poorly prepared, yet how powerful the sound when we are all well-prepared and well-tuned.

In the following chapter we will look at how we can help form our community of faith into a celebrating assembly. How are people transformed through participation in ritual and symbol? How does the community exercise its ministry in the celebration: gathering, listening, sharing, and being sent forth?

In Summary

1. The vision of the New Testament church was one in which the whole community, God's holy people, chosen and called, shared in the mission and ministry of Jesus.

2. Over the centuries this understanding was gradually replaced by divisions between sacred and secular, and lay and ordained. The active participation of the laity in the life of the church was reduced to that of passive spectators. These divisions remained in place until the Second Vatican Council.

3. The renewed theology of the Council brings out very clearly that ministry in the church is not for a chosen few. Christians, through their response in faith to God's call, celebrated in baptism, become the church. They participate fully in the church's mission to proclaim in word and sacrament the reign of God.

Discussion Questions

1. How do we continue to work toward the liturgical renewal called for by the Council?

2. How do we help the assembly, which includes all the baptized, understand its ministry?

3. How do we help those in particular ministries understand that all ministry flows out of the assembly and is not separate from it?

Forming
the Assembly

Liturgy is the action of the whole assembly, not particular individuals or groups. We are truly present and active in the celebration when "we involve ourselves meaningfully in the thoughts, words, songs, and gestures of the worshipping community—when everything we do is wholehearted and authentic for us —when we mean the words and want to do what is done" (*Music in Catholic Worship*, 3). How do we help the members of our assembly come to that "full, conscious, and active participation" called for by Vatican II?

Catechesis

The *Constitution on the Sacred Liturgy* indicates the need for "the liturgical instruction of the faithful and also their active participation in the liturgy both internally and externally, taking into account their age and condition, their way of life, and their stage of religious development" (*CSL*, 19). The formation of the assembly depends on parish priests and other liturgical ministers who need to "become thoroughly imbued with the spirit and power of the liturgy and make themselves its teachers" (*CSL*, 14). Therefore, one of the first steps in the formation of the assembly needs to be the formation of its liturgical ministers. We have to move beyond workshops that are mainly task-oriented, such as how to carry the lectionary, how to use a microphone, how to choose music, or how to distribute communion. Those who serve the assembly also need formation in theology, spirituality and liturgy.

The next step is liturgical catechesis for the whole assembly. All those who gather should understand the importance of their ministry. They should understand what they are doing and why they are doing it. This may take place in many ways.

Key moments

As Christians we turn to the church at various points in our journey through life. Parents come in contact with the church through the sacramental life of their children: baptism, confirmation and eucharist. As the children grow older, some will come to church to celebrate their marriage. We anoint those who are sick among us and we celebrate in prayer and ritual the passage of our members from this life into the heavenly kingdom. These are key moments when we can help people bring their life experience, their joys and their struggles to worship. For example, is baptism preparation in your parish the same for parents who bring their first child for baptism and a few years later their second, or third child? Sacramental preparation should take into account the context of the life situation of all who will celebrate this sacrament. Often our focus is only on the child. We should also acknowledge the life situation of the parents—helping them bring their life experience to prayer, to connect their own baptismal commitment with the baptism of their child. Perhaps a few months later it might be possible to gather the parents together for an evening of reflection on their experience of the baptism of their child and what baptism means for them as they continue their journey of faith.

Use the bulletin!

Parish bulletin inserts can effectively help members of the assembly come to a greater understanding of their ministry and how they can enter more fully into the prayer, gesture and symbol of the liturgy. Topics such as the liturgical year, the various symbols, prayers, gestures, objects, and sacraments could be addressed in short, informative reflections. Simple questions such as: Why did you come to church this Sunday? Why do we use incense during the mass? How do we celebrate Advent? Did you ever wonder why the priest kisses the altar at the beginning of mass? Who prays the eucharistic prayer? may pique the reader's interest.

The homily

Some would suggest that the Sunday homily is an appropriate place to educate people since they will not usually come to a session offered during the week. The General Instruction states that the homily "should develop some point of the readings or of another text from the Ordinary or from the Proper of the Mass of the day, and take into account the mystery being celebrated and the needs proper to the listeners" (*GIRM*, 41). How often have you heard a homily on the eucharistic prayer? One should be careful, however, that a reflection on a text or prayer from the liturgy does not turn into a lecture. The aim of the homily should be to help people come to a deeper experience of the presence of God in their lives and in their prayer, and move them to praise and thanksgiving; it is not just informative.

Involve the assembly in processes of change

Often, after careful evaluation, parishes change their liturgical space or pattern of worship without informing and involving members of the assembly. Too often changes have been made in parishes according to the personal tastes of the pastor or members of the planning team. This leaves people feeling frustrated and confused, often unwilling to participate. Times of change present an opportunity for catechesis. If you plan to change the way a community celebrates, ensure the whole community has a part in and understands what is happening. Parishioners need an opportunity to voice their concerns and discuss the issues. Such discussion and catechesis should take place long before the actual change. If there is a sound reason for making the change, most people will accept it positively. Involving the members of the community in the process lets them deepen their own faith, leading them to greater understanding and participation in the liturgy.

Celebrate well

The liturgy, when celebrated well, is also formative. It is an effective instrument in shaping the faith experience of the individual and the community. We recall Luke's story of the disciples on the road to Emmaus (Luke 24). The two disciples walked and talked with Jesus for many miles, but only in the breaking of the bread did they recognize their Lord and Saviour. The early church understood the power of the ritual experience in the lives of the people. For example, only after the catechumens had experienced initiation through the waters of baptism was the symbolic meaning of the ritual fully explained to them. When they looked back on their ritual experience, the catechumens began to understand its significance in their lives. The sermons during the Easter season used this liturgical experience of the assembly in order to help them understand the mysteries that they had celebrated.

There is an ancient axiom, *lex orandi, lex credendi*: the rule of prayer establishes the rule of belief. In the midst of the liturgical assembly we learn and experience what it means to be a Christian: what we believe and how we are to live our lives.

Hindrances to Formation

The culture in which we live can make hospitality, gathering and the active participation of the assembly difficult. In our materialistic society, moral and spiritual values are not as important as one's possessions. Our individualistic society assumes that the individual, not tradition or an institution such as the church, is the determining factor in setting values and standards for living.

Individualism affects the church and its worship. Many forget that our primary reason for gathering is to give praise and thanks for God's action in our lives. The goal of liturgy is not to focus on particular individuals or groups, or to satisfy their needs or desires. God must always be the primary focus and goal of the celebration. Individualism encourages people to establish their own religion. In creating their own religion, individuals are influenced by our consumer entertainment-oriented culture which measures good liturgy by whether a person feels good after the liturgy is over. This attitude contradicts the communal dimension of sacramental celebration.

The devaluation of the active role of the assembly is further aggravated by presiders and other ministers who allow individuals celebrating sacraments such as marriage, baptism, funerals, and ordinations to make liturgical choices based on their personal preferences. Recently, a church musician was overheard telling a bride-to-be not to worry about what was "liturgically correct"; it was "her day" and she could have anything that she wanted. Inappropriate choices, such as solo music or substituting a poem for a scripture reading because it seems more "meaningful," deny the assembly's active participation in the liturgy. This inattentiveness to the assembly's ministry encourages passivity and does little to fashion a channel for effective communication of God's grace within the celebration.

For or with people ?

We continue to do things *for* the people rather than *with* them. Therefore, many people come to liturgy with much the same attitude they had before the Council: to receive salvation or grace from the church. They do not know that they, the assembly, have something very important to do. Ministers who distinguish between "I" and "you" as in: "I would like to teach you the psalm response for this Sunday's celebration," or "Please sing louder, I can't hear you," reinforce the attitude that the assembly is a passive audience in need of encouragement.

We can offer liturgical catechesis in all its various forms, but if the assembly's worship experience contradicts what it has learned, this experience will have the greater influence. Everything that we do in our liturgical celebrations—every action, gesture, word, symbol, ritual, object, liturgical space—communicates a message, either positive or negative. Often this message is so subtle we are not even aware of it. But over time, it will shape and form the attitudes of those who gather. For this reason we must carefully evaluate our symbols, gestures, objects, liturgical spaces, how we gather, listen, share and are sent forth. (For more on this topic, see *Preparing and Evaluating Liturgy* in this series.)

Symbol

To enter fully into the celebration, the assembly needs to be well versed in the language of symbol. If we were to ask what the main liturgical symbols are, many would list the bread and the wine, the scriptures, the altar, water, and oil. How many would include the assembly? Most of us are not aware that "among the symbols with which liturgy deals, none is more important than this assembly of believers" (*Environment and Art in Catholic Worship* [*EACW*], 28). There must be an integrity in the symbols we use in our liturgical celebration. We need to understand how symbols operate within the worship of the church and why the renewal of the Second Vatican Council "requires the opening up of our symbols, especially the fundamental ones of bread and wine, water, oil, the laying on of hands, until we can experience all of them as authentic and appreciate their symbolic value" (*EACW*, 15).

The symbols employed in the church's liturgical action are not there to make us feel warm and fuzzy, but to draw us into the experience of God. In this sense, they can become unwelcome intrusions, confronting and challenging us to move beyond our present reality. At the same time, they can enable us to see and respond to the world in different ways. This new direction or focus prompts us to reflect on where we are and where we are going, enabling our participation in the sacraments to become a transforming experience.

Symbols help us discover the mystery of who we are, the essence of our deepest being. In doing so, we discover the God who lives within. Everything that is spoken, seen, felt, sensed, or acted out in the liturgy must draw us into an experience of God.

In classical Greek, *symballein* indicated something that effected unity. Initially a symbol denoted the part of a ring, plate or other object that had been broken off. The fracture line of both sections fit seamlessly. When friends parted, each would keep one section. These fragments were often passed on to their descendants. The fragments symbolized the permanence of the friendship and guaranteed recognition in future encounters.

When the two fragments were reunited, the friendship which only seemed to have been temporarily dissolved was symbolically restored. Therefore, symbols contain multiple levels of meaning, and can serve as a means of bringing human beings in contact with God.

Fundamental symbols such as fire, water, light, darkness, and oil have a long tradition in the church. Over the centuries, these symbols, when used as part of the church's worship, have retained their capacity to communicate different levels of meaning on a universal level. They are the result of both a long historical tradition, and the creative adaptation of cultural objects that express the transcendent. These symbols, when assimilated into the church's ritual, take on a different level of meaning.

However, symbols by their nature are open-ended, and express multiple dimensions of meaning at different periods. Consequently, time and cultural influences can obscure the original meaning of the primary symbols in worship.

Symbols communicate meaning and therefore the sign value of sacraments is important. For example, we speak of baptism as cleansing, as washing away sin. What will help the assembly enter into this image: a large amount of water, which can be seen and heard, or an insignificant dribble poured into a small bowl that can be neither seen nor heard? *Understanding the meaning is not enough!* Symbols must be allowed to embody the true and authentic spirit of the sacramental action.

We must ensure that the symbols we use are authentic. The traditional symbols of the church contain layers of meaning. Often our assemblies miss the link between the tradition and the symbol. For instance, we read the story of Noah and the ark that carried his family to safety during the great flood. From the New Testament perspective of our salvation in Christ, this story prefigures Christian baptism. Christian artists of the early church used the symbol of the ark to represent the boat of Peter, which symbolizes the church. How many people in our assembly would be able to look at a representation of the ark and see all these levels of meaning? We need to restore our Christian "story" to the assembly.

What happens when we use symbols that have no Christian foundation? For example, the butterfly is sometimes used to symbolize resurrection. Yet the caterpillar does not die; it undergoes a metamorphosis. It changes into a butterfly, with no resemblance to the original caterpillar. Jesus Christ truly underwent death. In the resurrection, he appears in his glorified body, recognizable by the disciples as the Lord who lived and walked and ate with them. How does the butterfly relate to this? How then does decorating with butterflies on Easter Sunday draw people into the Christian tradition of death and resurrection?

The symbolic activity of the sacramental celebration is the mystery of God's self-communication, continually inviting the participation of humanity in the divine life. This is communicated to the assembly through the actions and prayers of the liturgy. Consequently, the symbols used in the ritual of the church must be rooted in, and reflect, the church's faith and theological understanding of the sacraments.

Liturgical Spaces and Objects

How do our liturgical space and the objects used to decorate it help us to exercise our ministry of assembly? The liturgical space is symbolic of who we are and how we gather. Since the Council, many parishes have been faced with the problem of adapting or renovating their present worship space. Others have struggled with building new churches that will serve the needs of the people and the liturgy. With the assembly as a primary symbol we must look at our gathering spaces, the placement and seating of the assembly, the location of the altar and its relationship to the tabernacle. The renewed understanding of sacraments and the active participation of the assembly have led to questions regarding the placement and size of the baptismal font, its relationship to the table, the relationship of reconciliation to baptism and eucharist. Everything we use in our worship should lead us into the sacred and enable the active participation of the assembly.

Unfortunately, our society tends to what is convenient or inexpensive, using materials that only look like the real thing, such as artificial flowers and candles, material that looks like marble or wood. There must be an honesty and an integrity in our choice of space and material. The two demands liturgy makes on the arts are: "quality and appropriateness. Whatever the style or type, no art has a right to a place in liturgical celebration if it is not of high quality and if it is not appropriate" (*EACW*, 19). The things we use in liturgy must help to draw us into the mystery that we celebrate.

Using these criteria, how do we evaluate the objects that we use in worship? A simple example is the use of artificial flowers. What difference does it make if we use real or artificial flowers? Artificial flowers are cheaper. Since they never die, they may be stored and used over and over again. They are more convenient since you do not have to water them or pull off the dead leaves of flowers to keep them looking attractive. Opting for convenience reveals the subtle influence culture has on our worship. In everyday life, the people who gather on Sunday are immersed in a society that does all it can to deny the process of aging and death. However, we Christians are continually called over into the dying and rising of Christ, to die to ourselves, to live for others. Live plants and flowers can evoke our life, our growth, our decline and eventually our passage through death to new life. Scripture tells us that "unless a grain of wheat falls to the earth and dies, it remains just a single grain; but if it dies it bears much fruit" (John 24:12). On a very human level we also value real flowers since they will not always be there.

Does the liturgical space your community worships in invite it to gather, to feel welcome, to exercise its ministry? When we know someone is coming to visit, one of the first things we might do in preparation is clean the house. How often have you come to the last mass on Sunday to find bulletins and papers littering the pews from the previous celebration and the hymn books scattered all over the place? If hospitality ministers and ushers remained after the celebration it would only take them a few minutes to straighten up the worship space.

Can the people in the assembly see and hear what is going on around them? How is the space decorated? Often we decorate only the sanctuary area, highlighting the altar, chair and ambo. The area where the assembly is seated should receive the same care, visually reinforcing the symbolic nature and the ministry of the assembly.

As members of the assembly we need to understand that we have an active ministry in the celebration: in gathering, in telling our story, in participating in sacrament, and going forth to proclaim the reign of God in the world. When we listen attentively to the readings, when we respond, raise our voices in song, show care and reverence in our gestures and our postures, and extend hospitality to the stranger in our midst we are ministering to one another, sharing our faith in the risen Lord.

In Summary

1. To participate fully, to enter into the prayer of the li[...] members of the assembly need to understand the mear[...] the actions and symbols that form our worship.

2. The liturgy itself is an effective instrument in for[...] Christian assembly who understands and fully exerc[...] ministry. In the midst of this assembly we learn and [...] ence what it means to be a Christian.

3. For this reason we should carefully evaluate the actio[...] tures, words, symbols, rituals and space that form ou[...] gical celebrations.

Discussion Questions

1. What does your parish do to catechize the assembly?[...]

2. Does your liturgical space enable the participation [...] assembly? If not, what needs to be done?

3. Do the symbols and the way they are used help your [...] bly unite their lives with the mystery of the life, deat[...] urrection and coming again of Christ?

CHAPTER 5

"Full, Conscious, Active Participation"

rticipation in the ritual of the church is one way in which the
h community hands on its tradition. Coming together in
d and sacrament, the community shares in a common expe-
e and ensures that this faith is communicated and continu-
enewed from generation to generation. For this reason all
cramental rites are considered to be communal, rather
rivate, celebrations. The *Constitution on the Sacred Liturgy*
ds us that the people should be encouraged to take part
ans of acclamations, responses, psalmody, antiphons and
Through our common song, all respond to God who calls
ether in Christ (*CSL*, 30). Our common sung prayer is a
ry of praise and support. Our songs, prayers and gestures
s the faith within us, and enable us to share this faith with
other. This is why sacraments are celebrated in the pres-
f the faith community. The members of the faith commu-
turn, are called to take responsibility for caring for each

nce the Second Vatican Council, our goal has been the
conscious and active participation" of the people in the
ical celebration (*CSL*, 14). The key word is "conscious." All
ers of the assembly should be able to take part in the cel-
on, not because they are told to do something, and not by
nding automatically to the prayers and following the ges-
of the ritual, but by being fully aware of what they are
g.

Hospitality

The assembly should be encouraged to exercise its ministry of hospitality, which is fundamental to the worshipping community. Hospitality creates a space where all are welcome to come in and join, where strangers can meet without fear, and where, united in Christ, all become "one body." Hospitality sets the context for us to be able to really hear the good news, to feel God's gentle touch, and to freely use the gifts God has given us in the service of others. It is not only the hospitality ministers a the door who need to extend a greeting and make the strang feel welcome. It is the responsibility of the whole assembly reach out and pay attention to others.

Exercising our ministry of hospitality takes a consc effort. Do we recognize Christ in the person who sits next on Sunday? Where do we sit when we enter the church— end of the pew—or do we move into the centre to accomr those who come later so that they do not have to crawl o How often do we notice if there are sufficient hymn bo everyone? If there are not enough books, do we offer t ours with the person sitting next to us? Do we look into tl of those with whom we exchange the sign of peace ?

Those who extend hospitality never seek to exert over others. The most hospitable thing we can do for pe to pay attention and be present to them. In being hospit help to create a space where we can be open to God, oth ourselves.

Gathering

Called by God, the Christian community gathers to Sunday after Sunday in praise and thanksgiving. This ass gathered together as one body in Christ, is a sign of God ing will, of humanity gathered into one. Through the acti the liturgy, the assembly is strengthened in "their pow preach Christ and thus show forth the Church to those wl outside as a sign lifted up among the nations, ..." (*CSL*, 2).

Our gathering begins before we leave home on Su Knowing we are called by God, that we are a part of the munity of faith, makes going to church on Sunday a deliberate choice. Deep in our hearts we come to know that the assembling of our faith community is not complete if we are not present— no one else can take our place.

Understanding that we belong to a larger community helps us reach out to others as we greet people in the parking lot as we arrive and upon entering the church. It also helps us make the effort to be on time both out of respect for those who gather with us and in order to prepare ourselves for what is to follow.

We no longer enter the church in total silence, oblivious to those around us. However, the time before the liturgy begins is not there for us to plan the social agenda for the coming week, to decide where everyone will meet for brunch after mass is It is "sacred" time, time to become a "worshipping" assembly.

Before the liturgy begins, music ministers rehearse with the assembly those parts of the liturgy that might be unfamiliar. There is nothing more inhospitable than inviting the assembly to join in singing something it has never heard before and will have little chance of participating in. We need the tools to help celebrate as "one voice."

The *General Instruction of the Roman Missal* also emphasizes the importance of the gathered community (*GIRM* 7, 14, 25, Only after the people have assembled does the entrance begin, and the ministers enter. The primary purpose of the introductory rites is to create the opportunity for the assembly take on the form of a community and prepare themselves to listen to God's word and celebrate the eucharist properly" 14, 24).

Our ministry is to sing with full voice the gathering or opening song. Music draws us into a unity of voices and hearts. Music can speak to us in a way that words cannot. This moment of worship should express our personal and collective faith. We remain silent as the presider says "Let us pray." The ministry of the assembly is compromised when the presider does not allow enough silence for this prayer. This is our prayer—the silence helps us to formulate our interior prayer which, after a period of silence, is then "collected" by the presider into one prayer often called the *collect*.

Each member of an assembly that has truly gathered will help to lead the community as a whole into acknowledging its love of God. This gathering prepares us to celebrate our response to God's call through word and sacrament.

Listening

The introductory rites prepare us to listen to God's word. It unfortunate that, for many who gather, there is little expectati that the liturgy of the word will be a spiritual experier Printing the scripture references along with a brief commen in the Sunday bulletin may encourage people to prepare ten to God's word. The parish could also organize some fo Bible study to encourage people to study and reflect or ture as a group.

The assembly exercises its ministry during the liturg word by listening, responding, singing, silence and During the proclamation of scripture we are called to attentively to Christ speaking to us through the ministry reader. If we truly believe in the presence of Christ in the bly and in the word, we will not arrive late and expect to seat during the reading. Out of respect for the rest of the bly, ushers or hospitality ministers would ask those wh late to wait to be seated until the reading is over.

The sound of 1,000 missalette pages rustling simulta ly during a page turn announces that we are reading alon is very different from listening with open hearts. (Miss should be used *before* mass as a way of preparing.) To enc people to listen, lectors have to be well trained in the proclamation.

In the silence after each reading, we reflect on wha means in our life, what God is asking of us at this moment we pray for the needs of the church and the world. prayers express the active participation of the assembly, "the people, exercising their priestly function, intercede f humanity" (*GIRM*, 45). Once again we are called to take re sibility for our prayer. Do our prayers of intercession help us understand that it is not only God who feeds the hungry? We must take personal responsibility for what we pray for.

Giving Thanks and Praise

The fourfold actions of the eucharist are to take, bless, break and share. We begin as we would at home by preparing the table, then bringing in the food that will be shared by those who have gathered. Members of the assembly come forward with the offering of bread and wine—enough all present to share. In most places the collection ompanies this procession since the monetary gifts or the church and the poor. These are the f the whole assembly, to be shared by ole assembly.

the early church it was the prac- the faithful to bring the gifts of nd wine from their homes and e of carrying up the gifts retains me spiritual value and meaning" (*GIRM*, 49). parishes help to make this connection by having ers of the parish bake the eucharistic bread that will be at each celebration. Some parishes even have a group of oners who, following the *GIRM*'s prescriptions, make giving the assembly a strong identity with the gifts of nd wine used during the liturgy.

nen only a token amount of bread and wine is brought up procession, the subtle message is that the presider and union ministers may share the bread and wine that is rated at this celebration, but it suffices for the rest of the e to receive from the tabernacle. The symbol of sharing the ead, the one cup of blessing, which forms us into the one of Christ, is lost. A further implication is that the gifts the bly presented, "the work of human hands," are not tant or connected to this celebration.

e should also be careful to assure that our symbols are of quality that they can help us enter into the mystery that we lebrating. The *GIRM* tells us the bread should taste like

real food (283) and communion under the form of both bread
and wine is to be encouraged (240). How often does communion look like and taste like real bread?

After the gifts have been received and prepared we enter
into the great prayer of thanksgiving. Scripture accounts of the
Last Supper pass on to us that Jesus, taking bread and wine,
"blessed them" and "gave thanks," telling his disciples to do
this in memory of him. This is our eucharistic prayer. The Greek
word for this prayer was *anaphora*—to bear on high. This i
what we do—we are called to lift up our hearts and voices '
God.

Unfortunately many people experience this prayer a
long, often monotonous prayer recited by the priest. We nee
recapture the understanding that this prayer is an act of p
and thanksgiving of the whole assembly. The priest uni'
people with himself in the prayer he addresses in their r
the Father through Jesus Christ in the power of the
(*GIRM*, 54).

A unity of posture during the eucharistic prayer
help to unify the prayer. The wording of the prayer spe
standing: "we thank you for counting us worthy to st
your presence and serve you" (Eucharistic Prayer II). Sta
a traditional posture for prayer and praise, can encourag
of heart, mind and voice. Another way of maintaining th
of the prayer is through the musical continuity of th
responses. This means that the acclamations used shoul
the same musical thread running through them or, at th
least, be written in the same key and style.

We pray the "Our Father" and share the sign of pe
sign of our hope for "peace and unity for the Church, a
the whole human family" (*GIRM*, 56b). The breaking
bread should be done carefully and reverently—it "is a sig
in sharing the one bread of life which is Christ, we wh
many are made one body" (*GIRM*, 56c).

Consequently, eucharist is more than the transformat
the bread and wine into the body and blood of Christ; it i
the transformation of this gathered assembly—for we
prayed that "we, who are nourished by his body and b

may be filled with his Holy Spirit, and become one body, one spirit, in Christ" (Eucharistic Prayer III). We do not come forward as individuals but as a holy people called by God. The communion procession, therefore, is an act of the community. The communion song belongs to the community. It is not a choir or solo piece or time for instrumental music. The communion hymn begins when the priest receives communion (*GIRM*, 56 i). If this is truly a communal act there should be no division between the presider, communion ministers, and music ministers receiving communion and then providing something musical for the assembly. The communion hymn expresses "outwardly the communicants' union in spirit by means of the unity of their voices, to give evidence of joy of heart, and to make the procession to receive Christ's body more fully an act of community" (*GIRM*, 56i).

issal

ncements are made, a final blessing given, and the ly is sent forth to continue to witness to the reign of God world. Our work during this time is to read and pray with iptures, to celebrate the presence of Christ at our meals amily and friends, to try and bring reconciliation and o our communities and our world, to see Christ in each we meet, until once again we join together as "full, conand active" members of the Sunday assembly.

In Summary

1. The goal of liturgical renewal in our parishes should be the "full, conscious, and active participation" of the whole assembly in the church's worship.

2. An assembly who experiences the mystery of God and the power and presence of the risen Lord in its midst is open to all who come, sharing with them good news of salvation.

3. Through their participation in the celebration they w strengthen each other in the faith, incarnating God's heali and saving presence in their community and in the wo around them.

Discussion Questions

1. How is hospitality expressed in your parish?

2. How do you enable your assembly to exercise its min the gathering, the listening, the sharing, and the s forth?

3. Do the members of your faith community know tl coming together, by assembling for liturgy, they are a sacrament of God's presence in the world? That they primary symbol of the liturgy? What in the life of you munity would indicate this?

Conclusion

Our ministry of the assembly is fully realized in our daily lives, where we bring the presence of Christ and the message of the reign of God to the world. As members of the assembly, are we attentive to what the liturgy and other ministers call us to do? we pray and sing with full voice, do we listen attentively to readings, or do we fidget or talk and distract people around Do we allow the readings to challenge and confront us with message? When we say "Lord, hear our prayer" have we heard and taken to heart the people and the needs for we have prayed? Do our "Amens" ring out and fill the with the sound of our faith? Do we really listen to the tic prayer, do we remember and truly give thanks and Do we carry out our ministry with joy and enthusiasm? we truly entered into this liturgical celebration in such a at we have allowed God to strengthen and nourish us for ek ahead?

urgical celebrations are the prayer and
of the church. In answer to God's
community gathers to meet the Lord
symbol and action, word and sacra-
Our sacramental celebrations commu-
both God's revelation to human
and their free response to God's self-
nication. The liturgy is both a
celebration and a sacramental cele-
in Christ. God's unconditional love
ithfulness for his people is incarnated
s Christ. Christ, uniting in his person
he human and the divine, is the model
community. We are asked to die to self
life. Our mission, in response to God's
to help build the church into a commu-
f love that reaches out in service to the

BIBLIOGRAPHY

Recommended reading

Boyer, Mark G. *The Liturgical Environment: What the Documents Say.* Collegeville: Liturgical Press, 1990.

Challancin, James. *The Assembly Celebrates.* Mahwah, NJ: Paulist Press, 1989.

Dallen, James. *Gathering for Eucharist: A Theology of Sund Assembly.* Old Hickory: Pastoral Arts Associates of No America, 1982.

Fleming, Austin. *Preparing for Liturgy: A Theology and Spiritu* Chicago: Liturgy Training Publications, 1997.

Gelineau, Joseph. *Learning to Celebrate.* Washington, D. Pastoral Press, 1985.

Huck, Gabe. *Liturgy with Style and Grace.* Chicago: Training Publications, 1984.

Mauck, Marchita. *Shaping a House for the Church.* C Liturgy Training Publications, 1990.

Mick, Lawrence. *Worshiping Well: A Mass Guide for Plan Participants.* Collegeville: The Liturgical Press, 1997.

Ostdiek, Gilbert. *Catechesis for Liturgy: A Program fo Involvement.* Washington, DC: Pastoral Press, 1986.

Searle, Mark. *Liturgy Made Simple.* Collegeville: The Li Press, 1981.

"The Assembly," *National Bulletin on Liturgy.* Ottawa: Ca Conference of Catholic Bishops, Volume 24, Numl 1991.

Walsh, Eugene. *Giving Life: The Ministry of the Parish ʃ Assembly.* Daytona Beach: Pastoral Arts Associates of America, 1985.